James Davidson FGSI

Colourpoint

# Our Daily Bread, a look at Ulster bakeries

## James Davidson

*Dedicated to my father William, Pâtissier Extraordinaire*



6 5 4 3 2 1



Designed by Colourpoint Books
Printed by: The Universities Press (Belfast) Ltd

ISBN 1 904242 14 6

**Colourpoint Books**
Colourpoint House
Jubilee Business Park
21 Jubilee Road
Newtownards
County Down
Northern Ireland
BT23 4YH
Tel: 028 9182 0505
Fax: 028 9182 1900
E-mail: info@colourpoint.co.uk
Web-site: www.colourpoint.co.uk

The association between the Davidson family and the bakery business began in the late 1800s when the author's grandfather, also James Davidson, came to Belfast from Drumnamether, near Tandragee in Co Armagh. James is the third generation of his family to have worked in the bakery trade and joined the family business, the Eglinton Bakery in Belfast, in 1954.

His interest in the family trade knows no bounds and he has spent many happy hours researching the history of the many bakeries which once existed in the Province. The general public's interest in the subject has surprised him and he is now much in demand for speaking engagements at church associations and historical groups.

James is an Honorary Vice-President and Fellow of the Genealogical Society of Ireland.

Born in Belfast he now lives at Lambeg, near Lisburn.

Unless otherwise credited all photographs are by the author or taken from the author's collection.

**Front cover:** An Ormeau Bakery electric bread van dating from about 1958. *RHM Bakeries Ireland*

**Rear cover:** Left – 1920s Kennedy's advert, see pages 50/51 *Fr Hugh Kennedy*

Right – Ormeau Bakery breadserver, see pages 64/65 *RHM Bakeries Ireland*

# Contents

# Author's Introduction

I am of the third generation of my family to be involved in the bakery industry, which my father always referred to as the 'second oldest profession'. According to Genesis, chapter 40, verse 1, "The butler of the King of Egypt and his baker had offended their lord, the King of Egypt". The butler was freed but the baker was hanged!

Today, several millennia later, we still consume and enjoy the products of the baker – the breads, cakes and biscuits and some varieties, such as plain loaves, soda bread and potato farls, are peculiar to Northern Ireland. Veda bread is unique and the many varieties of cakes, such as iced diamonds, 'sore heads' and Paris buns, remain very popular.

Between the two World Wars these goods were supplied to nearly every household by mobile breadservers from the many bakeries in operation at the time. In the greater Belfast area there were about 25 bakeries and, with only one exception, all of these were family businesses. In the rest of the province there were about 30 bakeries and all were family-run establishments. A small number of these survived into the 1960s but have since closed or been absorbed by larger concerns.

In the following pages I will attempt to give the reader an insight into the general development of commercial bakeries in the province since 1850 and to highlight the most prominent establishments.

Most firms took a pride in their delivery carts and vans and indeed there were even competitions at various shows. Many of the vans carried the names of the families involved – Inglis, Hughes, Kennedy, Baine, McWatters, Parkes, Mercer, McComb and Gibson being examples – while others used company names such as Windsor (Patterson), Ormeau (Wilson), Eglinton (Davidson), Stewarts, Warwick, Marsh, Bloomfield and Granville. Times change and none of these families are working on the industry today. In fact Belfast now has just two bakeries – Mothers Pride and Sunblest.

Outside of Belfast the only family-run concern remaining is Irwin's bakery in Portadown. In Londonderry, familiar names such as Stevenson's, Eaton's, Brewster's, Hunter's and the Abercorn have all disappeared. Hunters also ran a family milling and bakery business in Limavady. Whaley's in Enniskillen was still in business up to the 1970s while, in Ballymena, Morton & Simpson's and the Bridge Street Bakery and Reid's Bakery in Coleraine have all long since closed.

McCann's Bakery in Newry was run by five generations of that family and Willis Bakery was one of the first to be absorbed into the Inglis group. Davison's Alexandra Bakery in Portadown was also taken into the Inglis group. Samuel McGredy, Snr, of rose fame, was once a director of the Alexandra Bakery. In the west of the province Russell's Bakery of Strabane and Doran's in Omagh were fine local concerns.

Probably the most fascinating and familiar part of this industry was the delivery of the products to the customer. Very few, if any, of the food industries manufacture and deliver their products direct to their customers' doorsteps. This phenomenon created a great institution of characters who, along with the horses and vans, have provided many stories, most emanating from the rural areas. As well as bakery products newspapers and magazines were also delivered and during the rationing of World War 2 the sale of products like butter, sugar, bacon and chickens provided those breadservers with a nice little supplement to their income.

Skills enhancement played a great part in the life of many bakers with many attending the bakery school at the Belfast 'Tech'; this school dated from the early 1900s. Many bakers owed their skills to the instruction received in that school and included amongst them were JB Kennedy and James Davidson, my grandfather. Both of these men subsequently became lecturers at the school. The Master Bakers Association provided an oven and equipment to assist the students. Competition was encouraged and in 1912 Mr George Inglis presented a cup for cake ornamentation. The school closed in 1940 but after World War 2 was revived, being set up in the former Millar's Jam Factory in Artana Street, Belfast. Day release classes for apprentices were held there until the new school was opened in the Belfast Institute of Further and Higher Education, Brunswick Street, in 1962

The Bakers' Guild in Ireland dates back to 1478, the first master being one John West and the trade union is still plays a great part in the industry. A pleasant little verse was quoted in Guild papers:

> Next comes the well-bred men, who know the way
> To please the ladies in their bread at tea,
> And with their white, their wheaten, and their brown
> Can please the palate of the lord or clown.

The local union was formed in 1873 and its first Secretary was Murray Davis. Its premises were in Curtis Street, off York Street and its name, the Bakers Friendly Society – a legacy from the combination laws which forbade a full trade union – was later changed to Belfast Operative Bakers and later still to the North of Ireland Bakers and Confectioners and Allied Workers Union. One of the best known Secretaries of the Society was Jimmy Morgan.

Bakery workers had their own club, imaginatively titled The Bakers Club, and many stories can be told about it; there are probably many more which can't! The club was situated above the Aero Bar at Bridge End in Belfast and was specially licensed to be open through the night for bakers who worked on late and night shifts. As far as I can ascertain, it closed in the late fifties or early sixties.

The range of local products, such as the plain loaf, the pan loaf and soda and potato farls, is familiar to all Ulster folk. Many similar products, though, are available in Scotland but one particular anomaly is the Veda loaf. The flour used in the manufacture of the Veda loaf was patented in 1904 by Robert Graham in Gleneagles, Scotland. The bread was popular in the early 20th century and was made in Veda bakeries throughout the British Isles. Today the Veda loaf is only made in Northern Ireland, although Veda Bakeries Limited exists in Glasgow.

My research has uncovered much information on the bakery industry in this Province and I hope you will enjoy the small selection of photographs and brief notes presented here. If any of the photographs or historical details jog your memory with a story or further information then I'd be pleased to hear from you. I may be contacted by writing to the publisher at the address on page 2.

James Davidson FGSI<br>Lambeg, Lisburn<br><br>November 2004

# The bakeries – a brief history

## Hughes' Bakery

Bernard Hughes was born in Armagh in 1808, the second child in a devout Roman Catholic family of eight children. At the age of twelve he went to work as a baker's boy in one of the town's bakeries. It was menial work and could have included delivering bread by handcart to local customers. Later he attempted a venture as a baker on his own account, but was unsuccessful. After working for a few years for another Armagh baker he decided to try his luck in Belfast. Eventually, at the age of eighteen, he found employment at the Public Bakery in Church Street and he was later appointed manager of the bakery.

By this time he had married Jane and they had a son, Peter. By 1840 he had set up his own company and within a few years was established as Belfast's leading master baker. He opened his newest bakery – the Railway Bakery at the corner of Fountain Lane in Donegall Place – in 1847. To get the produce from the bakery to the shop rails were laid the length of Fountain Lane. This site was very prosperous for 27 years. Milling flour was a natural business progression and he opened the Divis Street mill in 1877. The larger Model Bakery was built on the Springfield Road in 1884.

By the end of the century the business had become a public company and by 1930 the Hughes family had no involvement in the company. Changes in other areas led to it finally being wound up in 1979.

## Inglis & Co

The Inglis family was prominent in the sewed muslin trade in Scotland during the early half of the nineteenth century. James Inglis, Jnr, did not find this trade to his liking and, in his teens, he emigrated, not to London as many Scots had done before, but to Ireland and to its capital, Dublin. There he became associated with the well established bakery company of Johnston, Mooney and O'Brien. Some years in the business confirmed that this would be his career, although he had a preference for Northern Ireland.

An opportunity presented itself in the form of the business of John Trueman at 32 & 43 Castle Street, Belfast and James purchased it in 1871. Within ten years the shop in Castle Street was deemed to be too small and a site at Eliza Street, which had been occupied by the ironworks of Robert Hickson, the pioneer of Queen's Island Shipbuilding Yard, was acquired. By this time, 1881, James had been joined by his brother George. The business progressed and by 1900 occupied a site of approximately 2 acres. The company was incorporated as James Inglis and Company in 1894 and continued to expand by the acquisition of other local bakeries – Patterson Ltd, Windsor Bakery, William McComb Ltd, Snugville Bakery, Bloomfield Bakery Ltd, all in Belfast and TP Willis Ltd, in Newry. Tom Piggott had joined the company in 1937 by way of Brewster's in Londonderry and in 1937 the biscuit factory was opened. After World War 2 three more Belfast bakeries – City, Mercer's and McWatters – along with Davison's of Portadown were taken into the Inglis Group. In the late 1950s Brewster's of Londonderry was also absorbed by Inglis & Co shortly after the entire group was taken over by Rank, Hovis Ltd.

A new bakery – Milanda, Derry Ltd – was opened in Londonderry in 1966 and in 1969 the Milanda Bakery was opened at Apollo Road, Belfast. The Eliza Street site was closed and all production was transferred to the Apollo Road site, now known as Mother's Pride Bakery. The biscuit factory was closed in 1982 and although it still stands, the building has new occupants. Milanda, Derry was closed in 1992.

## Stewart's to Allied Bakeries

Joseph Lowry Stewart was born in 1881 near Crossgar, Co. Down, the eldest of five children. He left school at Barnamaghery at the age of 14 and came to Belfast; his first job was in a grocer's shop in Cromac Square. He married Catherine Christie in 1911 and in that same year he opened his first shop and bakery on the upper part of the Beersbridge Road in east Belfast.

The business was successful and as the sales of bakery products increased a new bakery was essential. This was opened in 1929 on the Greenville Road, also in east Belfast. With drawplate ovens, hot plates and a Scotch oven a wide range of bakery goods could be supplied to the Stewart's Cash Stores throughout Belfast and to other shop outlets. Progress was rapid and soon a total of 72 branches were being supplied. Thompson's Bakery in Ormeau Street was taken over, and in 1935 Garfield Weston came from Canada to look for a bakery in Belfast.

A deal was agreed, with Weston having the controlling interest and Joe Stewart as managing director. Tip Top Bakery became a strong brand and also the 'White Chief' logo was successful. Reid's Bakery in Coleraine was acquired in 1948 and this expansion created the need for greater production. In 1969 a new bakery was built in Coleraine and the brand name Sunblest became a market leader. Greenville Road was closed in 1984 and the Orby Link site was developed. In the third millennium Sunblest is now a world leader in the bakery industry.

Joe Stewart retired in 1951 and the grocery business was eventually absorbed by Crazy Prices (later Tesco) in 1985. He died in 1969, but is still remembered in the bakery world as 'Joe'.

## Ormeau Bakery

On 15 July 1868, having spent the day in Holywood, John Alexander Wilson and four friends were crossing Belfast Lough in an open boat, back to Whiteabbey. There was a stiff breeze rising and the light was fading. About 9.30pm their boat was capsized by the schooner *Harmony*. John Wilson and two of his friends – Mr William Grant and Mr Chisholm – were drowned. Their bodies were not recovered for some days.

John A Wilson had a bakery at 38 Great Edward Street, Belfast (now Victoria Street), and was involved in a partnership with David H Strain in a bakery at the corner of May and Cromac Streets, where Telephone House is today. Following John's death his brother Robert stepped into the business but the partnership did not succeed and he later moved to 88 Cromac Street trading as Robert Wilson, Baker and Flour Merchant. His son, James Elliott Wilson, was born there in April 1877.

A new partnership between David H Strain and William McCracken Wilson developed from 1865 at the Cromac Street bakery and progressed successfully until William McCracken Wilson's death in 1920. DH Strain had previously died in 1904. William Wilson became a city councillor and alderman for the Cromac ward.

By a strange coincidence in later years the two Wilsons, although not related, lived in adjacent houses in Hampton Park at the top end of the Ormeau Road. Robert Wilson prospered and eventually built 'Ava House' – the beginning of the present Ormeau Bakery. The construction of the Ormeau Bridge in 1862 enabled that side of Belfast to develop beyond Ballynafeigh. The business grew rapidly and in 1907 his son James became Managing Director. With his brother Samuel he led the Ormeau Bakery to became a very successful company. Perfection was the byword and they recorded many 'firsts' in the bakery world – the first to make soda bread, previously a domestic product, the first travelling hot-plate to bake soda and potato farls, the first to wrap bread in Ireland and, in 1971, the first bagged bread in Northern Ireland. In 1935, it was the first bakery in Ireland to have fleet of electric bread vans.

Unfortunately during World War II food rationing had a disastrous effect on the bakery industry, so the Ormeau Bakery did not make cakes or wrap bread. After food restrictions were withdrawn the company farm at Kirkassock near Moira, Co Down, made a great contribution by providing milk, cream and butter from the prize-winning herd of Jersey cattle. Eggs from the free-range chickens were used in cake making. Ormeau Bakery products were exported all round the world as the company developed in the hands of Ian Wilson as Managing Director and his cousin Elliott Wilson, who was in charge of the bakery.

In the early 1980s the food industry was in the throes of many changes – not all for the best – and Isaac Andrews & Co Ltd bought control of the bakery. There were many other factors coming into play and in early 2002 Mother's Pride Bakery took over the Ormo brand.

## Stewart's Royal Bakery

In 1903 George Stewart was a bread-server with Patterson's Windsor Bakery, Lisburn Road, Belfast, having previously spent seven years with Robert Jardine & Co. in Queen Street, Belfast. During that year he took over bakery premises on the Ravenhill Road, and the Royal Bakery was established. He was active in many fields such as Willowfield Church and was a city councillor from 1924 to 1928. His two sons John and George were involved in the business but, in 1933, the 'bread price wars' were raging. The business was to be sold but it was rescued by Samuel Brown, his father-in-law, who had a grocery business on the Woodstock Road. Although George Stewart, MBE, died in June 1945 his sons carried on the business until it was taken into the Inglis Group in 1959.

## Eglinton Bakery

James Davidson, of Drumnamether, Co Armagh, came to Belfast in the late 1800s where he worked in bakeries and possibly in the Ormeau. About 1920 he started on his own in a bakery on the Old Lodge Road, Belfast, opposite Eglinton Street. The business developed and my father, William J Davidson, joined the family firm in 1921. Larger premises at 37 Lisburn Road were ideal for expansion as there had been stables for horses. The bakery was expanded and the third generation of the family (me!) became involved from 1954.

The Carlton Restaurant in Donegall Place was taken over in 1948. Further expansion meant a takeover of Warwick's Bakery in Felt Street, off Sandy Row and Baine's Bakery, Montrose Street. A new bakery at Springfield Parade was built in 1961 but in 1962 control passed to Isaac Andrews Flour Mills.

## Baine's Bakery

There was a George Baine in the Larne area in 1854 – a grocer and miller with connections to Glynn Mills. He was a master baker and his brothers were bakers, too. He was successful and disposed of the business to Messrs Wilson & Strain, Ltd, Belfast, having been appointed managing director of that firm. Subsequently he recommenced business in his own name in Montrose Street, Belfast, around 1914. This venture was prosperous and involved his four sons, David, Cecil, William and Ronald. George died in October 1931 and the four sons were all active in the firm – particularly David who, at a later time was involved with Veda flour. He was also well-known for his golfing prowess. In 1960 the business was taken over by the Eglinton Bakery.

## Marsh & Company

John Marsh served an apprenticeship in Carr's of Carlisle to learn the biscuit trade. In 1862 he came to Belfast and was a partner with Joseph Ferran in a bakery making ships' bread and biscuits. Business was good and in 1873 he was joined by his brother Joseph Chandler Marsh who had been apprenticed to a firm of architects and builders in Darlington. By 1881 a site was selected for a new bakery 'at the hill in Donegall Street', at the junction of Carrick Hill. McLaughlin & Harvey was the main building contractor along with Combe, Barbour & Combe. The building, a large part of which still survives, was a superb example of Annadale brick and terracotta work . The two brothers enjoyed success, in spite of two fires, and, as members of the Society of Friends, were involved in various charitable bodies. Joseph, for example, was the Chairman of the Royal Victoria Hospital.

Unfortunately John Marsh died in 1891 at the relatively young age of 50. His brother Joseph died in 1913 and both are buried in the

Friends' Burying Ground at Stockman's Lane, Belfast. Following the demise of the brothers there were many changes of directors and management. The company was reformed to become Marsh & Co. (1928) Ltd. The Donegall Street factory was closed and production transferred to the former Springfield Cotton Spinning Mill to be known as Springfield Biscuit Works. The business continued and in 1949 Scribbans Kemp, an English company, took over the firm and continued trading until 1960 when it closed. The name Scribbans Kemp was later taken over by Barker & Dobson. The buildings were ultimately demolished to make way for the Springmartin housing site.

Their products were excellent and the best known was the Niagara Cracker, the original name for the Cream Cracker and was the first cracker biscuit made in Ireland.

## JB Kennedy Ltd

The Kennedy family was engaged in different businesses in Lurgan during the 18th century. James was born in 1815 and founded the High Street bakery about 1835. His sons John, James and Joseph were also involved in the business. Although trade was good James Bernard Kennedy came to Belfast and set up the well known family company. His sons James and Hugh carried on the business into the 1970s when the bakery merged with Bernard Hughes, who had also taken over Eaton & Co of Londonderry. Isaac Andrews had a major share holding in a new company, Peter Pan Bakeries. The Kennedy Bakery and Hughes' Factory on Springfield Road were closed in 1976 and production transferred to Ormeau.

## Irwin's Bakery

Irwin's Bakery was founded in Portadown in 1912. It was a family business dealing mainly in groceries but the demand for bread offered a market for a wider range of goods. The bakery was sited in Obins Street and trade increased at a superb rate. A fine range of products and a delivery service contributed to the success. In 1963 some innovative work by Bob Mowbray, the production manager, and a bakery engineering company from Leeds produced the square potato farl to change this aspect of bakery production. As the Obins Street site became too cramped a new location was necessary. The new bakery was opened in 1995, the first bakery to be built for many years. In 1990 Irwin's expanded their interests by taking over McCaldin's Bakery in Monaghan. This of course led to a wider market. Then in 1996 they took over McCann's Bakery in Newry and this was followed by a takeover of Lavery's Bakery in Monaghan. Irwin's is now the largest family-run bakery business on the island.

## Hugh Stevenson & Co

This company was founded by Hugh Stevenson in Waterloo Place, Londonderry in 1840. Steady progress meant a move to William Street. A wide range of products was made, including fancy breads and biscuits. The upper floors of the premises were used as drying rooms for ships' biscuits and for a type of coarse biscuit much in demand in Donegal. Confectionery was also manufactured and a restaurant business catered for the local market. John, Hugh, David and Isaac Stevenson, the sons of the founder, carried on the business for many successful years but the inevitable changes in methods of production in the 20th century had dire effects. The bakery was taken into the Ormeau Group in the early 1970s.

## The Model Bakery, Londonderry

The Model Bakery, James Street, Londonderry was opened in 1872 although the business was founded in 1863. The biscuit bakery was of a very high standard producing fine wafer biscuits. The Brewster family remained in control of the business until Inglis & Co took control in 1960.

## Rock Mills, Londonderry – Samuel Gilliland & Sons Ltd

These mills were built as flour and meal mills in 1846 by Samuel Gilliland and were successfully operated by his youngest son Mr RK Gilliland. In the early 1880s the introduction of roller mills, which replaced the traditional millstones, brought many changes including greater output and varieties of flour.

The Rock Biscuit Co manufactured bread, cakes and biscuits. The business was later taken over by the Hunter family who also had bakery and milling interests in Limavady. The Rock Bakery closed and the building was later renovated for use as student accommodation.

## McWatters's Bakery, Cromac Street, Belfast

John McWatters opened his bakery in 1880. It was originally on the east side of Cromac Street but moved across the street to larger premises in 1885. John's two sons, Gordon and Jack, later joined their family in the business. During the 1920s and 1930s McWatters were known for the fine horses used to pull their bread carts. They were taken over by Inglis and Co. in 1954.

## Whaley Baking Company, Paget Square, Enniskillen

George Whaley opened a shop on the High Street in Enniskillen in the 1890s. His son Cecil, born in 1897, was to become the driving force behind the business. After World War I he was joined by his brother Tom. The main part of their trade was over the border and after 1922 they had to rebuild in Fermanagh as tariffs were imposed by the Irish Government on imported goods in an attempt to protect local industry in counties Cavan, Monaghan, Leitrim, Sligo and Donegal. In 1929 the business moved to Paget Square. The other residents of Paget Square were able to cook their turkeys in the bakery's draw-plate ovens on Christmas Eve. During World War II contracts to supply bread to British and American Army Camps kept the bakery working at full pitch. Some weeks they used more than 300 gallons of buttermilk to make soda and wheaten bread. In 1948 Cecil's son, Junior, joined the company and then Derek also returned to Enniskillen in 1974. In 1991 the Department of the Environment vested the bakery site for redevelopment. The Whaley Bakery Co moved to a site at Killyhevlin Industrial Estate where it continued to trade until 1995.

In January 1953 Junior Whaley was in London at a packaging exhibition. He was accompanied by two young men from Belfast; they were Spence and Lennox Piggott, sons of Tom Piggott of Inglis & Co. They were due to fly back to Belfast on the Friday, but the weather was foul, the flight was cancelled and they were offered tickets to travel by rail and steamer via Stranraer and Larne. Junior decided to stay in London for the weekend. His two friends travelled aboard the *Princess Victoria* and were lost at sea.

## United Co-operative Baking Society, Ravenhill Avenue, Belfast

This was the bakery division of Cooperative Wholesale Society which was controlled by Glasgow and Manchester offices. Between the two world wars the Co-operative movement was very strong and they had many grocery stores in Northern Ireland and a large department store in York Street, Belfast. They also had a bakery in Enniskillen. The advent of supermarkets made many changes and the bakery closed around 1980. The premises, a fine brick-fronted building on Ravenhill Avenue, lay idle for many years but has now been redeveloped into an apartment complex – Bakers Court.

# The bakeries in pictures

A. & J. McCANN,

Wholesale & Family Grocers, Wine, Spirit & Provision Merchants,

*Plain and Fancy Bakers and Flour Merchants,*

28 & 30 HILL STREET,

**Bakery and Stores, Castle Street,** NEWRY.

This sketch shows McCann's Bakery which was located at Hill Street in Newry. As can be seen, the family provided more than just bakery products. Five generations of the family were involved in the business, which was eventually taken into the Irwin's Group. Part of the Victoria Bakery remains today and will form part of a heritage centre in the near future.

Like McCann's in Newry, Irwin's in Portadown also ran a grocery business, which had been its main market. The bakery department eventually took over and is now operating from a new factory unit on a local industrial estate. These premises were in Obins Street and the man wearing a leather apron, standing in the gateway, was probably a yard man. His duties would have included looking after the horses and carts.

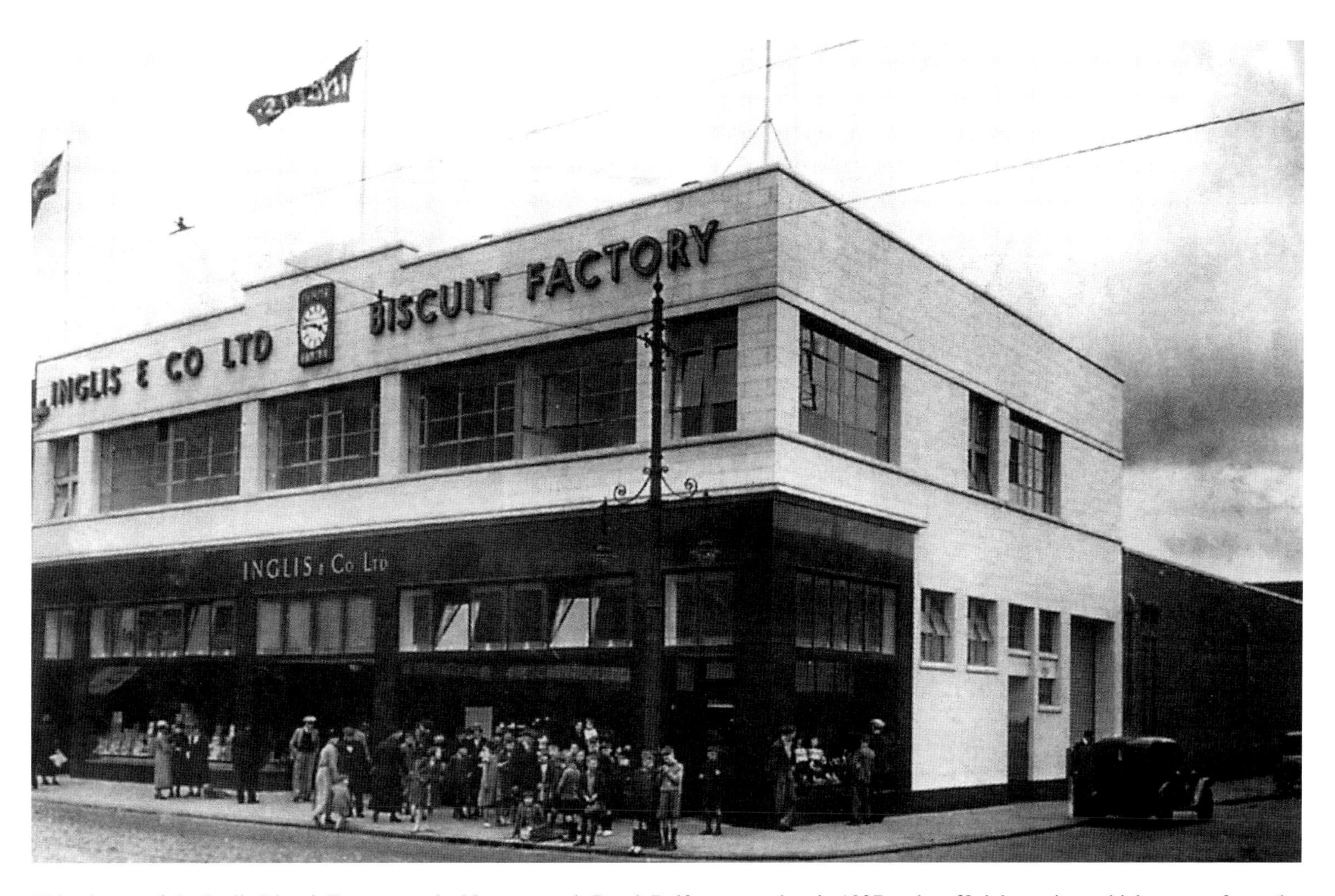


This picture of the Inglis Biscuit Factory on the Newtownards Road, Belfast, was taken in 1937 at the official opening, which was performed by the Lord Mayor of Belfast, Sir Crawford McCullough, Bt DL. The factory is said to have cost £100,000 and was the most up to date biscuit factory in Ireland at that time. Note the children waiting outside. Were they guests at the opening? Were you one of them?

Production ceased in 1980, as competition from larger manufacturers in England and Scotland became stronger.

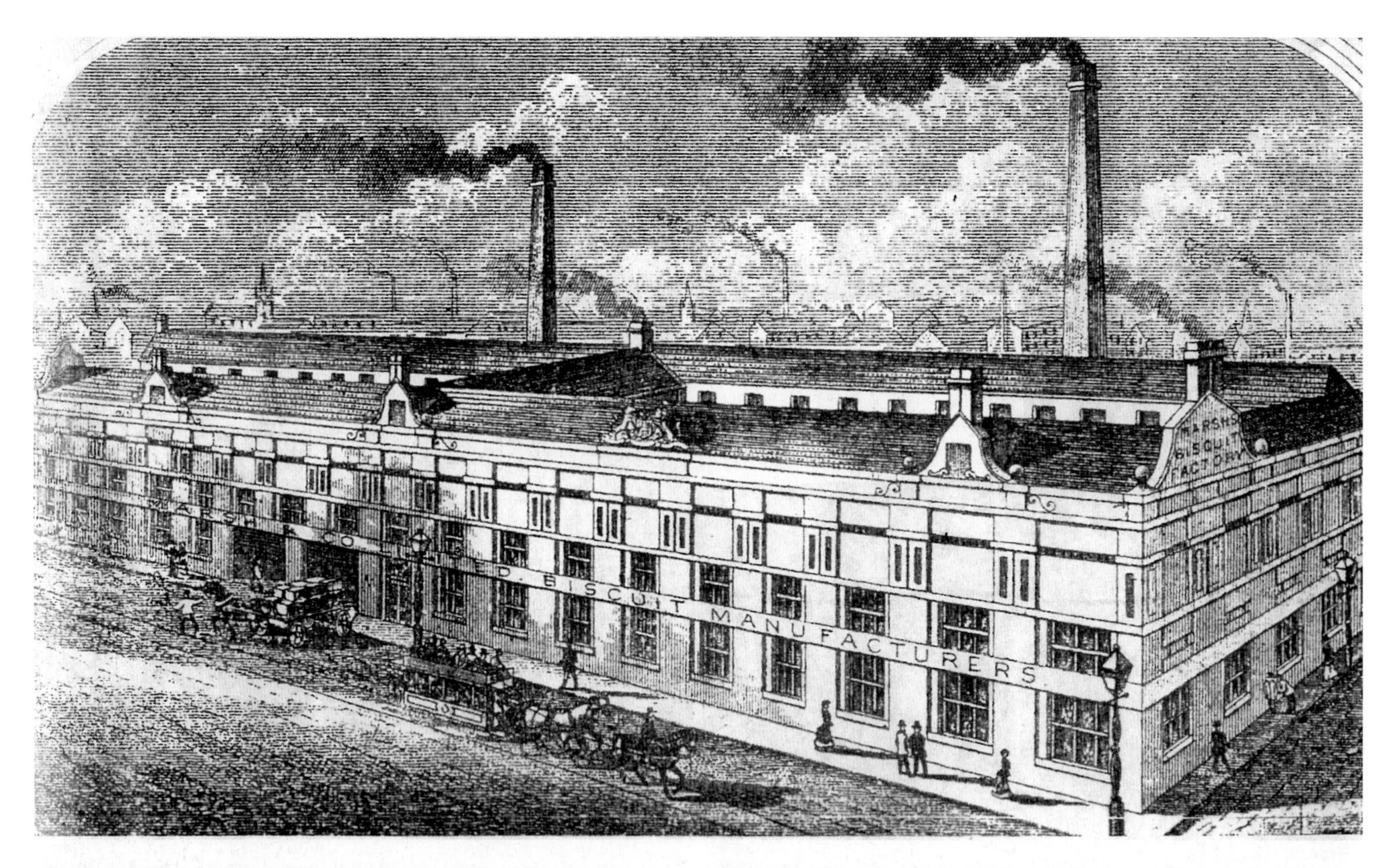


**Above:** No photographs of the Marsh & Company Biscuit Factory in Donegall Street, Belfast, can be traced but this sketch dating from the 1880s shows well the size of the building, which was built of Annadale brick, with terracotta work. The premises were vacated in 1949, yet in 2004 a large part of the building still stands.
The Annadale Brickworks mentioned above was located on the Annadale Embankment, at the end of Ava Street. The site is now covered by houses.

**Right:** McWatters's Bakery, Cromac Street, Belfast was founded in 1880 but it was on the opposite side of Cromac Street to the building in this photograph. The business was taken into the Inglis group in 1954, the premises being demolished in the early 1970s.

*Environment and Heritage Service,*
*Department of the Environment in Northern Ireland*

M'WATTERS'S BAKERY LTD. ESTABLISHED 1880
RKE BROS
CIALS 135
SOLD
BY
K
Kinnaird

**Left:** This photograph, from the collection held at the Public Record Office of Northern Ireland, shows the premises of Messrs William McCracken Wilson and David H Strain, at the corner of May Street and Cromac Street, Belfast, in 1885. Mr Strain is pictured with Miss Gilmore and Miss Frobisher. Strain's first partner John Wilson, who died in a drowning incident in Belfast Lough in July 1868, was no relation to William McC Wilson but was connected to the family who founded the Ormeau Bakery. The Strain family were also involved in the linen business and had a warehouse in Bedford Street.

David Strain had come to Belfast from Saintfield in 1860, as had William Wilson. Strain died in 1904 and Wilson in 1920.

*The Deputy Keeper of the Records,*
*Public Record Office of Northern Ireland*
*(D/2585/17/3)*

**Opposite:** This photograph shows a delivery of flour being made to the Whaley Baking Company, Paget Square, Enniskillen in 1936. Whaley's was a fine example of a provincial family business but unfortunately it succumbed to the pressure of the supermarkets and big groups. The premises were eventually demolished and an old people's home now stands on the site.

The truck is an Armstrong-Saurer, built under licence by Armstrong Whitworth at Scotswood-on-Tyne in the northeast of England. Saurer vehicles were originally produced in Switzerland and had a reputation for strength and reliability, something which would seem necessary given the load that this truck was carrying. Back in 1936 a journey by road between Belfast and Enniskillen would have taken between five and a half and six hours! *Cecil (Junior) Whaley*

THE WHALEY BAKING Co
BELFAST
CZ3410

**Above:** This building in Ava Street housed the Transport Department of the Ormeau Bakery and was originally a stable block but later housed vans and offices. It was demolished in the 1980s and there is now an apartment block on the site. This picture has been dated to about 1945. Note the air raid shelter to the left side of the building.

*RHM Bakeries Ireland*

**Opposite:** The Davidson family who owned the Eglinton Bakery also owned the Carlton Cafe and Restaurant in Belfast's Donegall Place. The Carlton was responsible for the catering at Government House, Hillsborough, and in 1956 was awarded a royal warrant for this work. The warrant was presented to the author's father, William J Davidson, JP.

The site in Donegall Place is now occupied by Oasis Fashions.

o. 29
Carlton Cafe & Restaurant
CARLTON CAFÉ AND RESTAURANT

# Owners and personalities

**Far left:** George Findlay Inglis was born in Scotland in 1836. He came to Belfast in 1881 to partner his elder brother, James, in the business of James Inglis & Co. This business was successful and both brothers prospered. George had a son, J Norman Inglis (born 1887), who after attending university and distinguished service in the army during the First World War, returned to his duties as a Director in the bakery in 1919.

George Inglis died in 1924, one year before his elder brother, James.

**Above:** The gentleman on the extreme left of the picture is George Stewart, MBE, proprietor of the Royal Bakery, Ravenhill Road, Belfast. Stewart had worked for Patterson of the Windsor Bakery, Belfast, before starting his own business in 1903. His sons, John and George, later joined the company. Stewart was also a member of Belfast City Council from 1924 to 1928.

This posed photograph shows sandwiches and cakes being packed for a function, possibly a church outing or Orange demonstration.

*Noel Brown*

**Left:** These gentleman are the four Baine brothers. Willie (in front) was the administrator, Ronnie was the accountant, Cecil was the engineer and David (at the back), the baker, who was also very well known for his golfing prowess. Willie eventually married one of the McWatters girls after an engagement lasting more than ten years!

*Helen Henderson*

James Elliott Wilson was born in April 1877 at 88 Cromac Street, Belfast. He became Managing Director of the Ormeau Bakery in 1907 and was the driving force who really put it on the map by setting exceptional standards for quality and service. He died in 1956.

*The Wilson Family*

These gentlemen are members of the Whaley family, of Enniskillen baking fame. All three were deeply committed to their business and to the life of the County Fermanagh town. Derek is on the left of the picture with Cecil (Junior) on the right and their father, also Cecil, inset. Cecil senior and 'Junior' always worked in the business but Derek spent some time working in the textile trade in West Africa.

*Cecil (Junior) Whaley*

# The bread making process

**Left:** This is a typical Ulster kitchen hearth and members of the older generation will be familiar with the crane and griddle. Oatcakes would have been baked on it and also soda and potato farls. This would have been normal practice before loaf bread was available. Other features to note are the harnen stand for warming oatcakes and the salt box fitted on the wall to the left. *RHM Bakeries Ireland*

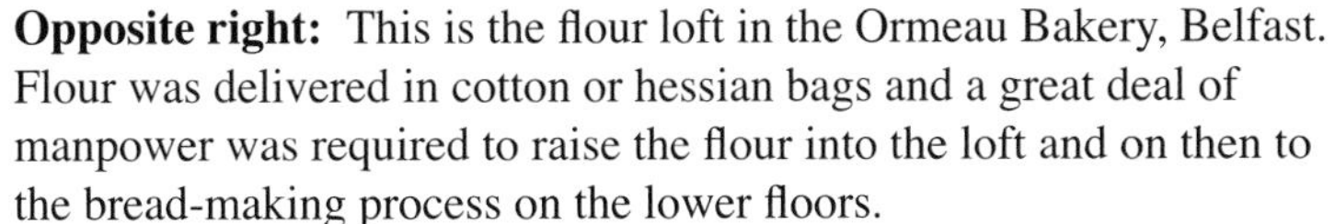

**Opposite right:** This is the flour loft in the Ormeau Bakery, Belfast. Flour was delivered in cotton or hessian bags and a great deal of manpower was required to raise the flour into the loft and on then to the bread-making process on the lower floors.

*RHM Bakeries Ireland*

**Above:** This 1905 view of the Ormeau Bakery, shows the dough mixers in the background with the wooden troughs where the dough was left to ferment, lined up in sequence. These wooden troughs were later replaced with stainless steel. *RHM Bakeries Ireland*

**Above left:** In the 21st century things are much different with deliveries being made by bulk tanker, 25 tons at a time – no spillage and not a grain wasted. Consequently the manpower involved is considerably reduced and therefore the process is more efficient.

These are drawplate ovens, so called because the drawplate, or sole, is drawn out on the floor on a wheeled carriage. These particular ones were coke fired, which produced good bread but the process was very labour intensive. Note the plain (batch) bread just removed from one of the ovens. This view dates from 1932. *RHM Bakeries Ireland*

This is the drawplate oven at Brewster's Bakery, Little James Street, Londonderry in about 1910 and it is loaded with batch bread. Brewster's was a well known family business which continued production into the 1960s, after being taken over by Inglis and Company in 1958. They also made a fine range of biscuits. The drawplate oven is loaded with batch bread. As mentioned previously, the baking process was labour intensive. Look how many people are involved here for a relatively small amount of bread. *David Bigger collection*

Over the years the production process for making bread has become more mechanised and less labour intensive. Even back in the 1930s machinery was being developed to make the job easier. This machine, in use at the Ormeau Bakery in 1935, automatically measured the precise amounts of flour and water required for batch bread dough. It still required some human input but now even that has almost gone, the whole process being computer controlled.

*RHM Bakeries Ireland*

In 1935 the Ormeau Bakery's bread plant was 'state of the art', producing a high quality product efficiently and effectively. This photograph shows conical moulders, which shape the dough pieces prior to final moulding and proving then baking.

*RHM Bakeries Ireland*

This is the dough making plant and in this view is under the control of Harry McIvor. His was a responsible job, ensuring that the dough was to the correct consistency and that it was delivered in a steady flow. The continuous dough making plant was designed by Campbell Brown.

*RHM Bakeries Ireland*

Soda bread is extremely popular in Northern Ireland but do you know how it gets its distinctive shape? Well this is an early soda pinning and cutting machine. It was designed and built by Campbell Brown; he was a genius of an engineer in the 1920s. He produced equipment that enabled bakers to offer soda farls in greater quantities than was possible by using the old fashioned griddle.

*RHM Bakeries Ireland*

The first travelling hotplate in the Ormeau Bakery was installed in the late 1920s and was used for the production of pancakes, crumpets and pikelets. Basically similar systems are still in use throughout the United Kingdom over 80 years later.

*RHM Bakeries Ireland*

We all take wrapped or bagged bread for granted. This was an early design bread wrapping machine, dating from the mid 1920s, which used waxed paper. The waxed paper was often reused to wrap 'the piece' taken to work. The use of paper was discontinued during World War II, only resuming in 1948. Later plastic bags and clear wrapper were introduced.

*RHM Bakeries Ireland*

Team spirit is vital in a process job and these men – Doug McDowell, George 'Juker' Irwin, Billy West and Billy Hunt – appear to be enjoying their work, moulding fruit loaves, in the Ormeau Bakery in the late 1970s. Men working together as a team usually developed a good working relationship.

*RHM Bakeries Ireland*

Bread products must be allowed to cool before they can be wrapped. This piece of machinery is a cooler for soda farls. (It is normally enclosed but has had the covers removed for the photograph.) The farls are placed on a mesh conveyor and cool air is passed through the unit as the product moves towards the wrapper. The ability to cool products quickly meant that goods could be wrapped, and ultimately despatched, more promptly.

*RHM Bakeries Ireland*

The pancake, in its many styles and flavours, is obviously popular in Ulster households. Using a travelling hotplate, about 10,000 pancakes per hour can be produced. Even in this photograph almost 200 can be seen. The network of pipes on the side carry the gas used to warm the hotplate.

This machine was a variation on the travelling hotplate shown opposite being used for the production of soda and potato farls. One side was baked on the outward journey then the farls were turned, manually, and the other side was done on the way back. Note the distinctive shape of these soda farls.

This is an Artofex dough mixer in operation. A bowl of dough mix is wheeled under the mixer (note the trolley), the safety door is closed and the mixing process begins. The bowl rotates during the carefully timed process and on completion the bowl is removed to the next stage, a replacement bowl being inserted and the process allowed to continue.

Once the dough is mixed and ready, the baker cuts out large pieces of dough which are fed into a divider. This machine cuts the dough into loaf-sized pieces. The manual element of this process has now been superseded, as the bowl is mechanically tipped into the divider.

The loaf-sized pieces are then roughly shaped on a conical moulder, seen in the background, by the window. In some cases this may be done twice to ensure a well-shaped loaf.

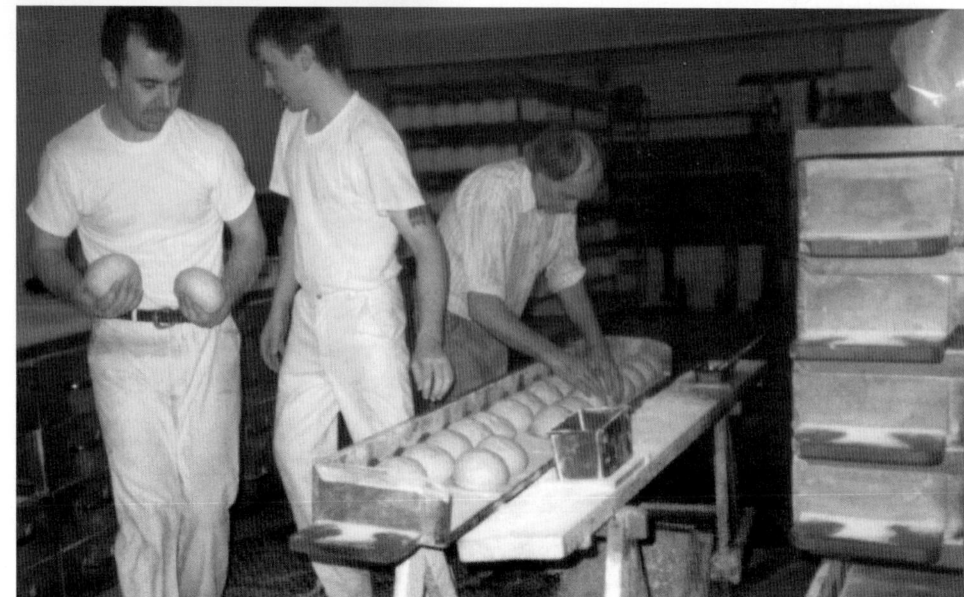

The rounded pieces are then placed on setter trays. Between these stages the dough is allowed to recover from the mechanical handling which helps the even rise of the loaf during baking.

The next stage is to set the rounded pieces on the drawplate oven. This picture was taken in Lavery's Bakery in Monaghan. John Lavery is on the right of the picture. A good technique in this process ensures a good, even, well-risen loaf.

John Lavery and his son, Patrick, complete the full oven batch of 40 dozen loaves. The plate is then rolled into the oven and after 45 minutes the result is a batch of beautiful loaves.

Having been in the oven for some time, the bread is very hot and care has to be taken when removing, or 'stripping', the loaves on to racks to cool, prior to slicing and wrapping.

Modern bakeries use tunnel, rather than drawplate, ovens for producing batch bread. This is a much more efficient method and the throughput is obviously much greater than that of drawplate ovens as it is a continuous process.

The method of stripping the batch bread from a tunnel oven is similar to the drawplate process. The tunnel can be up to 100 feet long and the speed of the belt, or oven sole, can be set to suit baking time, depending on the size of the loaf.

The loaves are cooled mechanically and then bagged after slicing. During these processes handling is minimised and the product is well presented and ready for sale.

Although, in this 1935 view, the Ingredients Store at the Ormeau Bakery looks a bit bare, many materials other than flour were used in cake making. The Ormeau Bakery always placed great emphasis on the fact that they only used the very best materials – including milk, cream, butter and eggs from its own farm near Moira – and the use of their own laboratory enhanced this claim. Note the Del Monté tinned fruit, a brand name still familiar in 2004. *RHM Bakeries Ireland*

# The workers

This photograph shows a group of Ormeau Bakery Staff and is dated 1891. James E Wilson seated on extreme right. The date is dubious as James, who was born in 1877, would have been 14 in 1891 and appears much older. *RHM Bakeries Ireland*

We move on 15 years to 1906 and another group of bakery staff at the Ormeau. Unfortunately no names are available for this photograph – possibly someone could offer some clues? It is just possible that the gentleman on the back row, to the right of the photograph, is my grandfather, James Davidson.
*RHM Bakeries Ireland*

In 1939 Baines Bakery, Montrose Street, Belfast celebrated its 25th anniversary and this group photograph was taken as part of the celebrations. Although many staff were included no members of the Baine family feature nor do any of their bread servers.

**Above:** This picture was taken in the Bakery School in the 'Tech' in Belfast in 1918 and features (second from left) George Stewart of the Royal Bakery, whom we saw earlier on page 21. The occasion could have been a presentation day but there is neither information about the young man holding a certificate nor the names of the other bakers. *Noel Brown*

**Opposite, left:** This advertisement for The Ards Flour & Bread Company appeared in a *Belfast Street Directory*, dated 1915. It is interesting to note that despite being located in Mill Street they milled their flour in Belfast.

**Opposite, right:** Marsh & Co must have been confident of the quality of their cream crackers as they included a guarantee in every packet.

# Getting the message across

*Advertisements.*

THE ARDS

## FLOUR & BREAD

COMPANY,

MILL STREET,

NEWTOWNARDS,

Have been in existence for Nine Years, and have succeeded far beyond their anticipations.

They continue to turn out Bread of the very Finest Description, and as the Flour is manufactured at their own Mills, Belfast, perfect purity is guaranteed. Steam Machinery is extensively used in the Baking operations, thus avoiding personal contact as far as possible. Strict attention is paid to the cleansing of all vessels used in the various processes.

For Sweetness, General Quality, Weight, and Value, their Bread is unsurpassed.

**JAMES FLETCHER,**

MANAGER.

This is one of a series of adverts for Inglis' bread which appeared in the *Belfast Street Directory* during the 1920s. There was a common theme – the harvest – and the message was that Inglis' bread was a healthy food that would keep you strong.

In the early 1900s Veda bread was baked all over the United Kingdom. Although it is still a very popular loaf over 100 years later it is now only baked in Northern Ireland.

This newspaper advert dates from the 1930s.

GEORGE BAINE,

Bread and

Biscuit Manufacturer,

MAIN STREET,

LARNE.

☞ Fancy Bread and Pastry Baker.

Soirees and Parties supplied on
Moderate Terms.

This simple advertisement for George Baine, bread and biscuit manufacturer, appeared in the *Larne Times* during 1895. George Baine moved to Belfast in 1914 and set up business there.

*At last,*
*the Bread*
*that* **WILL**
*Satisfy.*

*Please Phone 7801, or send a P.C. and our van will call for trial order.*

Have you seen our Prize-Winning Turn-out at Balmoral Show? Perhaps you have not seen our Bread recently? If not, why not try it now? The kiddies will love it. Baked entirely from the FINEST FLOUR and INGREDIENTS procurable, in the LATEST and MOST UP-TO-DATE recently installed OVENS, the QUALITY is now UNSURPASSABLE. You can always be certain that the Bread you get from our Bakeries is perfect through and through, from crust to crumb. And every loaf is equally fine . . . equally delicious . . . and equally fresh.

BERNARD HUGHES, LTD.
MODEL BAKERIES - - - BELFAST.

Another 1930s advert, this time for Bernard Hughes' Model Bakeries in Belfast. Note the four-digit telephone number and the request to 'send a P.C.' (postcard) if you would like a van to call for a trial order. In the safety conscious days of the 21st century would advertisers be allowed to encourage young children to slice bread

**Above:** This is a photograph of a metal advertising sign for Marsh & Company's biscuits. It was most probably made in their own tin works in Donegall Street where the biscuit tins were manufactured.

**Opposite, left:** This advertisement for Inglis's is taken from a Unionist publication dated about 1929, hence 'The Bread for Ulster' slogan. A good illustration of the bakery in Eliza Street, Belfast features.

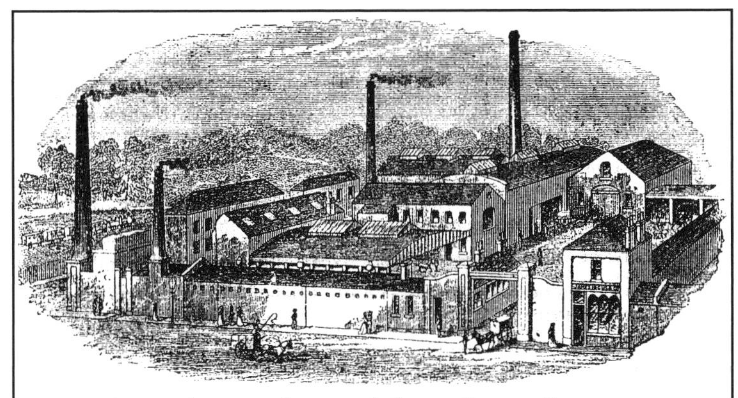

JAMES INGLIS & COMPANY'S STEAM BAKING FACTORY.
33 & 35, Eliza Street, BELFAST.

The BREAD for ULSTER:

· INGLIS'S ·

ADMITTEDLY THE BEST.

COLOUR, FLAVOUR, AND KEEPING QUALITIES UNRIVALLED.

*NOTE.—Railed to all the principal Towns in the North of Ireland.*
AGENTS WANTED IN UNREPRESENTED DISTRICTS.

JAS. INGLIS & CO., Ltd.,
BELFAST.

**Right:** The Ormeau Bakery was obviously proud of its technological achievements in both the production and delivery of its bread, as this *Belfast Newsletter* advertisement from 1940 shows. One hundred vans lined were up for this photograph in Park Road at 7.30am on 27 May 1937 before setting out on their rounds.

BREAD

OF PROVED MERIT.

LONDONDERRY.

**Alexandra Bakery,**

**PORTADOWN.**

We Supply all kinds of

PLAIN and FANCY BREAD.

Our Vans make Deliveries inside a radius of Ten Miles of Portadown. 'Phone or write for Van to call.

*Support Local Industry.*

**DAVISON BROTHERS, Limited.**

'Phone—Portadown 40.

**Above:** This advertisement for Davison Brothers' Alexandra Bakery appeared in a 1921 issue of the *Northern Whig* as part of a campaign to promote business in the Portadown area. Note that deliveries were only made within a ten mile radius of the town as this gave a suitable round trip mileage for the horses.

**Left:** Eaton's of Londonderry won an award at the Confectioners, Bakers and Allied Traders Exhibition in London in 1926 and used this very simple advert to spread the word to the good citizens of the 'Maiden City'. A depiction of the medal awarded, featuring Ceres, the ancient Italian goddess of tillage and corn, was included in the advert.

NUTURA
REG.D
Made only by Inglis & Co Ltd., Belfast.
A NUTRITIOUS & APPETISING FORM OF WHITE BREAD
Manufactured by a special process

**Above, left and right:** Inglis's 'Nutura' proved to be a successful product, possibly as a result of the good advertising of a quality bread. Note that it was delivered wrapped, unusual for the time in itself, in 'dust-proof paper'. The advert on the left is actually a postcard – a novel form of advertising – and dates from 1915.

*Left: Francis Dickson*
*Right: Author's collection*

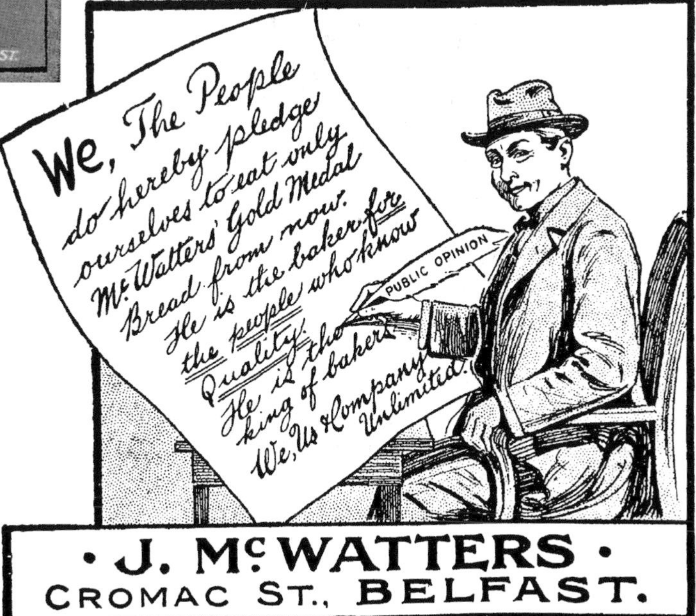


**Right:** This advert for McWatters 'Gold Medal' bread dates from 1912 and is a play on Lord Carson signing the Ulster Covenant in Belfast City Hall on 'Ulster Day', 28 September 1912.

Ormo

TRADITIONAL IRISH
OATCAKES

perfectly pure . . .
perfectly delicious

Ormo Oatcakes are baked by a carefully controlled method giving a round biscuit type Oatcake which is uniform in size and thickness. The traditional recipe containing no animal fat, produces a delicious flavour not to be found in any other product, while their crispness and freshness are ensured by packing in specially designed airtight cartons and packets. Ormo Oatcakes, for long popular locally, are now selling particularly well in Scotland, England and as far afield as the United States and Canada. They are delicious with butter, cheese, preserves or savouries.

*Please send for descriptive folder and address of nearest stockist.*

**ORMEAU BAKERY LTD.**

**BELFAST BT7 3GN**

**Opposite left:** This very simple but effective advertisement for Kennedy's Bakery dates from the 1920s. The size of the loaf does seem somewhat exaggerated, though.

*Fr Hugh Kennedy*

**Opposite right:** The Ormeau bakery produced this advertisement during the 1960s to promote its Irish Oatcakes. It is worth noting that this particular product was being exported to other parts of the United Kingdom, Canada and the United States of America.

*RHM Bakeries Ireland*

**Right, above:** McComb's Bakery was one of the first companies to advertise its products on Belfast's trams. This picture is dated 1904, not long before Belfast's tram services were electrified. Note here the trace horses which would have been attached to assist the tram horses on the long climb up Ligoniel Hill.

*The Deputy Keeper of the Records,*
*Public Record Office of Northern Ireland*
*(LA7/26/JC&JD)*

**Right:** Of course, the obvious place to sell the benefits of your product is on the side of your delivery van. Here we see two Tip Top Bakeries employees standing alongside their van, which is extolling the virtues of the 'White Chief' loaf – hygenically sliced and wrapped!

Tip Top Bakeries later became Sunblest.

# Delivering the product

**Opposite:** 1919 and McComb's breadserver Robert Morrow makes a delivery to Ellen Irvine at Ballymoran, Co Down. As can be seen from the loaves in the back of the cart, most bread at this time was delivered unwrapped. In rural areas newspapers and magazines were also frequently delivered by the breadservers.

*Wesley Geddis*

**Above:** This early 1930s photograph shows the Dispatch Department of the Ormeau Bakery, probably at the end of the day as there is little bread on the racks and the carts appear to have been washed out.

*RHM Bakeries Ireland*

**Left:** Here we see George Stewart with some members of staff at the Royal Bakery, Ravenhill Road, Belfast in the late 1920s. Mr Stewart was always well dressed; note he is wearing a bowler hat which showed his managerial position. *Paul Stewart*

Some of the smaller bakeries also had their own bread carts for local deliveries. One such was the Woodvale Bakery. This was likely a family concern and no doubt took a great pride in their products. The location of the bakery hasn't yet been traced but could have been in north Belfast.

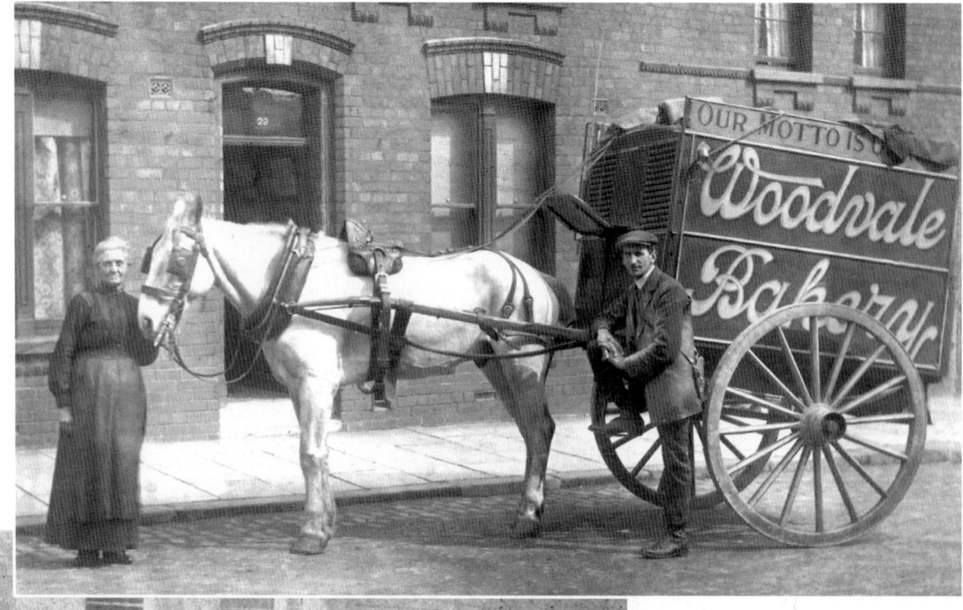

This photograph of a Newtownards Co-operative Society Ltd bread cart dates from the early years of the 20th century as evidenced by the panel proclaiming 'Best plain loaf in Ireland – Dublin Exhibition, 1903'.

The company's registered address was 2 Frances Street, a site now occupied by an office of Halifax Estate Agents, so where once you could buy your daily bread you can now buy a home!

*John Hanna collection*

In prewar years there was a competition at the Balmoral Show for horse drawn carts. Many trades competed – coal carts, milk carts, in fact any company who used horse power – and carts and horses were always smartly turned out. This bread cart belonged to Davidson's and is seen here on Belfast's Ormeau Embankment, en route to the show in 1933. Davidson's was renamed Eglinton Bakery Ltd in 1935. The man in the white coat is Mr John R Davidson, an uncle of the author.

Improvements to bread carts included bogie steering and pneumatic tyres, both of which made life much easier for the horse. One problem with earlier wooden wheeled carts was getting the wheel stuck in the groove of the tram rails but with pneumatic tyres this obviously wasn't a problem. This view of an Eglinton Bakery cart is dated 1936.

This was the stable block of the Ormeau Bakery. The horses walked up a wooden ramp to the stalls on the first floor. All the carts were housed at street level. After the horses had gone, the motor vans used the ground floor and the upper was used for storage and offices. The building was eventually demolished to make way for apartments in the 1990s. *RHM Bakeries Ireland*

Fourteen of Baine's Bakery's carts can be seen in this view of the covered yard at Montrose Street, off the Newtownards Road, in east Belfast. Baine's was one of only two bakeries to use white-painted carts, the other being Parkes and Co who operated from Byron Street, off the Oldpark Road in the north of the city. *Helen Henderson*

Local agricultural shows were popular places to display bread carts and bakery products as throughout the 1920s and 1930s they were always well attended events. Local competition ensured that both horses and carts were well turned out as in the case of this Stevenson's of Londonderry cart.
*David Bigger collection*

**Left:** This cart belongs to Morton & Simpson's Bakery, Ballymena. The photograph is dated 1951 and, if the date is correct, this must have been one of the last carts in operation. The bakery closed in the 1980s. The two gentlemen are Alex Ritchie (seated) and Charles Manson, holding *Tip-top*, the horse.

*Mary Goodrich*

**Below:** This is one of the first motorised vans operated by the Royal Bakery, Belfast and is possibly a late Ford Model T dating from around 1926. The young man in the picture is John Stewart, son of the proprietor, George Stewart.

*Paul Stewart*

The building on the right of the picture was originally Gilliland's Bakery and Mill, and was located on the west bank of the Foyle in Londonderry. It later became Hunter's Rock Bakery; it is now student accommodation. The vehicles seem to have been prepared for a show, the Napier van claiming to be Derry built. Its registration number (UI 617) indicates that it was the 617th vehicle registered in Derry City.

Alongside is the mixed gauge track of the Londonderry Port & Harbour Commissioners which ran from Graving Dock through to Foyle Road. A bogie wagon can be seen to the left of the picture. *David Bigger collection*

This custom-built Ford van was operated on a country route, around Ballycastle, in the early 1920s. Boyd's Bakery was established in Ballycastle in 1847 by Hugh Boyd with a capital of £5. The bakery was still in operation in the 1950s by Alex Boyd.

*Tommy McDonald, Impact Publishing*

Local shows and fairs were good places to promote your products and here we see a Stevenson's van dressed overall for the show in Londonderry. Stevenson's were later taken over by the Ormeau Bakery. *David Bigger collection*

**Right:** This picture shows the van fleet of McKeown's of Lisburn in the early 1950s. McKeown's was a family business which was started in 1852 and continued through three generations until 1986 when it closed. The shop is still open in Sloan Street in Lisburn, as a general store and is noted for its homemade ice cream.

*Mavis Heaney*

**Below:** This photograph by AR Hogg shows a line-up of electric vans in Park Road, Belfast, opposite the Bakery. It was taken at 7.30am on 27 May 1937 and was used in many advertisements after that date.

*RHM Bakeries Ireland*

In the days before motorways the quickest way to deliver the bread from the Belfast bakeries was by rail. The photograph shows an empty Inglis container on its way back from Portadown in 1961. For the benefit of rail buffs the locomotive is Ulster Transport Authority No 99 *King George VI.*

*Charles P Friel*

Although a successful method of delivery to rural areas, the closure of the railways in the west of the Province brought the era of bread containers to an end. Here at Omagh, in July 1964, we see a 6 wheel flat wagon with a container belonging to Stevenson's of Londonderry. *Charles P Friel*

The closure of the railways and the consequent loss of the use of containers meant that the bakeries had to look to other means for the bulk delivery of their product. This was the Ormeau Bakery's first articulated bulk delivery vehicle. The trailer, which was fitted with racks for rear and side loading, was hauled by a Guy Otter tractor unit and was new c1952. Most journeys by this type of vehicle were at night or in the early mornings. *RHM Bakeries Ireland*

ORMO
WZ 8642

**Left:** A scene that will be remembered by many is this one of the breadserver delivering from his electric van. This photograph, showing a van well packed with their wide range of products, was used by Ormeau for advertising. *RHM Bakeries Ireland*

**Above:** Time marches on and the electric vehicles were replaced by petrol/diesel models such as the Bedford CF seen here. This one had bodywork by Wrights of Ballymena, now better known for building high quality, low floor buses for the UK, US and Hong Kong markets. The van illustrated is no doubt long since scrapped and Supermac, Belfast's first out of town shopping development, has disappeared under the Forestside site. This photograph is believed to date from c1981 and the salesman has been identified as Sam Kelly.

*RHM Bakeries Ireland*

This early model electric bread van, believed to have been new in late 1938, is seen leaving the yard at Hughes' Springfield Road, Belfast, premises. One of Hughes' vans, similar to this, has been preserved and is on display at the Ulster Folk and Transport Museum, Cultra, Holywood, Co Down.

*Belfast Telegraph*

Later models of Hughes vans, both petrol and electric, are shown here being packed by their drivers before setting out on their rounds. Note the sliding canopy on the older vans while the newer, petrol one on the left uses the van door to provide protection for the salesman. All the goods are well packaged.

*Belfast Telegraph*

**Right:** This picture shows the original stable building at the Ormeau Bakery in about 1937 but with motorised vans instead of carts. This photograph is one of the few remaining images of this era. Compare this view with the one on page 56, when horses reigned supreme.

*RHM Bakeries Ireland*

**Left:** Competition in the city before the arrival of the big supermarkets meant the van salesmen had to show off their products to their best possible extent and to as wide a market as possible. Kennedy's used this specially adapted Commer van with a display window built into the side (see general view overleaf). *Fr Hugh Kennedy*

**Overleaf:** Although the photograph is undated it is believed to be about 1961, judging by the vehicle registration. The layout of this vehicle was unique at that time and how successful it was is not recorded. Note the range of breads, biscuits and cakes that would have been available from the van salesman. *Fr Hugh Kennedy*

COMMER
BREAD
CAKES
Kennedy's
BREAD
7808 XI

This Bedford lorry dates from about 1959 and was used for the bulk delivery of bread to shops and depots. The bodywork is believed to have been constructed by local coach-builders, Harkness, although the front of the vehicle appears to have been made up using parts from a contemporary Duple coach. The location for this picture is Orby Link, Belfast, where the headquarters of Sunblest Bakeries is now situated. The Sunblest logo, which was in use throughout the UK, is evident. *Allied Bakeries Group*

This battery powered van was delivered to the Eglinton Bakery around 1952. It had customer access at the rear and a hot water hand wash facility for the salesman. A special vehicle at the time, it became redundant with the advent of the supermarkets. Note the vehicle licence plate below the front nearside door.

The young man in this Austin Seven van is Carl Hinnerick, Jnr. His father, Carl, Snr, hailed from Germany and was a superb baker with a very successful business in Bangor. He later opened further shops in Bangor, Donaghadee and Belfast under the name Ca'dora, named after his daughter, Dora. Interestingly the sign writing on the van is for The Ca'doro, a slight difference in spelling. *Peter Radcliffe*

# Events and occasions

This picture records a visit by Lord Carson, James Craig and the Lord Mayor of Belfast, James Johnston to the Bakery School at the 'Tech' in Belfast, during 1918. Bread and cakes made in the bakery were supplied to patients in the Somme Hospital, which had been established at Craig's former home. Note the UVF hampers on the shelf at the back. Lord Carson is standing to the right of the table, with his hand resting on it and the tall man standing two behind is Francis Forth, Principal of the 'Tech'. JB Kennedy is just to the left of the white-tiled structure.

*Charles Ludlow*

Believed to have been taken around 1919/20 (because of the Martini rifle carried by the police constable), this photograph shows bakery staff and their families about to set off on a summer outing from the Royal Bakery, Ravenhill Road, Belfast. Apart from the two charabancs – a Thornycroft, running on solid tyres and a Daimler – the fashions are worth noting. George Stewart is in the centre, in the lighter coloured suit. In the charabanc, immediately to the right of Stewart, is Mr S Brown. The presence of an armed policeman is of interest and gives credence to the date. A second constable is standing by the wall beyond the charabanc. Note, too, the tram lines and the square setts. *Noel Brown*

**Above:** The Ormeau Bakery was probably the only bakery in Northern Ireland to have a Home Guard unit during World War II. This photograph shows the Officers and NCOs. Standing, left to right are Joe Bittle, Walter Ruddell, Hector Hartley, James Neill, Tom McCullough, Ernie Maxwell, Tom Mullan, Joe Briggs, William Coils, Bertie McDowell, Hugh Dickson and Bob McConnell. Seated, left to right are John Magill, James Dodds, John Montgomery, Tom Burrows, James McCaw, Cyril Quigley, Ted McCartney, Bob Stephens and Harry Kinnin.

*RHM Bakeries Ireland*

**Right:** This picture records the participation of CW Hart, the world champion long distance runner, in the 1914 London–Brighton run. The man in the car is Mr R Graham, the patentee of Veda Bread. Mr Graham seems to have realised the value of sports sponsorship early! *James Kerr*

**Above:** This picture was taken at a luncheon in the now demolished International Hotel, Belfast in 1964, to celebrate the Championship victory by the Bakery School team at the competition in London the previous year. Seated from left are Ken Brew, John Scarborough, David Baine and John Lyttle. Standing, extreme left is James Morgan of the Bakers' Society and extreme right Jim Kennedy. The author is third from the left.

**Above:** Mrs Gordon Neill (Neill's Flour Mill) is seen on a visit to the Bakery School, Belfast in 1965. John Scarborough, no doubt discussing the finer points of cake baking and decoration, was the senior lecturer in the school. *Neill's Mills*

**Left:** A visit to the Ormeau Bakery by Lord and Lady Wakehurst is recorded here. Ian Wilson, Managing Director, is in the centre of the photograph and the baker is Tom McCullough who also appears in the picture top left. *RHM Bakeries Ireland*

# Miscellaneous

BAINE'S BAKERY

(G. BAINE, Proprietor.)

IRISH CHAMPIONSHIP

WON IN COMPETITION,
LONDON EXHIBITION, 1913,

For the Best Bread (all classes included) made in Ireland.

G. BAINE has made bread to win no fewer than ELEVEN FIRST PRIZES at the London International Exhibition.

No other Irish baker can lay claim to more than five firsts, and no Belfast baker to more than four firsts.

BAINE'S BREAD can now be obtained in Larne, THE HOME OF ITS ORIGIN, the Larne Department being under the direction of Mr. D. LUKE, who is ready and anxious to supply every Larne man with

BAINE'S BREAD.

**Above:** Prize winning was an attractive form of advertising. All bakeries competed throughout the years and cake decoration was a popular form of displaying ones skill. As there are so few bakeries now the competitions have been discontinued.

**Right:** The business which later grew to become the well known local supermarket chain Stewarts began trading at the end of September 1911. This advertisement appeared in the local press.

OPENING ANNOUNCEMENT.

JOSEPH L. STEWART

Begs to notify that he has taken over the business recently carried on by Mr. DAVID YOUNG at

9 Greenville Terrace, Bloomfield,

and intends opening on

SATURDAY, 30th SEPTEMBER, 1911,

With a Fresh and Select Stock of

General Groceries and Provisions,

at Lowest Possible Prices for Cash.

SPECIAL VALUE in TEAS at 1/4, 1/8 and 2/- per lb.
BEST CRYSTAL SUGAR, 3d. per lb.; 2 lbs., 5½d.

FLOUR! FLOUR! FLOUR!

2d. per st. less than usual retail prices.

Good Baking Flour ... 1/6 per st.
Very Best Flour ... 1/8 „
New Oat Meal ... 1/10 „
Finest Wheat Meal ... 1/6 „
Finest Whole Meal ... 1/8 „
White's New Season's Flake Meal (in packets) 6½d. per ¼-st.

Finest Crean Butter and Fresh Irish Eggs at lowest market prices.

Brown & Polson's Corn Flour, 3d. per lb.

Washing Soda, 6d. per st.

Sunlight Soap, [illegible] lbs. for 5½d.

Hudson's Washng Powders, 9d. per doz.

3d. Tin Wood Milne Boot Polish for 2d.

BEST VALUE EVER OFFERED TO THE PUBLIC.
A TRIAL RESPECTFULLY SOLICITED.

NOTE ADDRESS

Greenville Cash Stores, 9 Greenville Terrace,

334 UPPER BEERSBRIDGE ROAD, BLOOMFIELD.

This is one of the two original mill-stones at Neill's Flour Mill, Belfast. This is the running (top) stone, ie the one that turned, and was in use for almost 120 years until milling ceased in 1985. When new office accommodation was built in 1986, the stone, cut from French Burr stone, was built into the office wall to show the continuity of the milling business on this site in the centre of Belfast. The bed stone (lower) is now at the restored corn mill at Castleward, Co Down.

*Barney Hughes's bread,*
*Sticks to your belly like lead,*
*Not a bit o' wonder,*
*You fart like thunder,*
*Barney Hughes's bread.*

**(Belfast Street Song)**

This picture was taken at Killyleagh, Co Down around 1930. The location is believed to be Frederick Street and the building in the background was the corn store, long since been demolished. The breadserver, who worked for McComb's Snugville Bakery, is Mr Willie Burns and the young lady is Miss Annie Neill, later Mrs Jordan.

*Martin McCloy*

Flour was delivered to the bakeries in hessian and cotton bags. Many of the hessian bags were return to the millers for re-use but the cotton bags were used for many other purposes, particularly in times of scarcity, such as during the two world wars.

The size of the bags was important. The 140lb bag (in bakery measurements two 140 lb bags represented one sack) when unstitched, opened out flat and sewn to another made a double bed sheet. The print on the cotton was not always easy to bleach or wash out. A story is told of a lady who made bed sheets in this fashion but when placed on the bed the print read 'Heart's Delight' (Oldlum's Flour) on one side and 'Magnificent' (Rank's Flour) on the other! There were also many uses for the cotton bags in the home – backing for handmade quilts and curtains and, in the kitchen, jelly bags and cloths being examples.

It is said that Distillery Football Club jerseys were made from cotton flour bags, hence their nickname – 'The Whites'. In County Kildare in the 1920s the local team used flour bags and were nicknamed 'The Flourbaggers'. They later used bags from Shackleton's Mill that had a printed name of 'White Lily Flour' and even today the Kildare team is named 'The Lily Whites'.

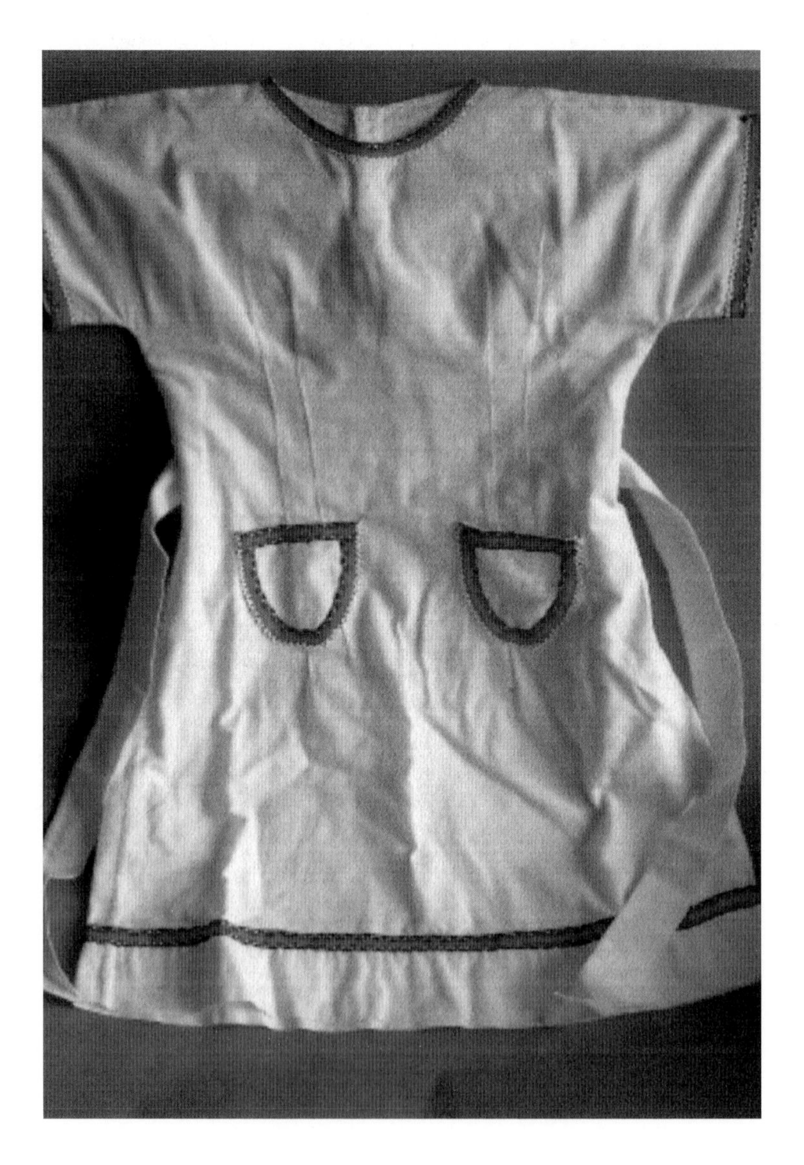

Bakery tokens and Ormeau breadservers badge

**1 and 2** Nothing is known of the purpose of these tokens although they could have been an early form of 'token collect' promotion. The endorsement on one side is 'Patterson's Belfast, bread and rich cakes', with an image of George III on the reverse
**3 and 5** This token was issued by Hughes's, Belfast and appears to have a value of 1 farthing. The significance of the title 'Railway Bakery', which was located at the corner of Fountain Lane, is unclear.
**4** This Bernard Hughes sixpenny bread ticket was dug up in a garden in Dunmurry in the 1990s. It is believed that this and item 3 would have been given by Mr Hughes to people begging him for money.

This smartly turned-out gentleman is an Ormeau Bakery breadserver. Note the badge, of the type illustrated at No 6 opposite, on his lapel. His horse, too, is smartly turned-out – well brushed, with harness and brasses brightly polished.

# Acknowledgements

This book could not have been published without the assistance of the following people and institutions who provided photographs and much historical material.

Institutions:
Bakers, Food and Allied Workers Union
Central Library, Belfast
Linenhall Library, Belfast
MAGNI
Mitchell Library, Glasgow
Public Record Office of Northern Ireland

Newspapers & Periodicals:
*Belfast Telegraph*
*The British Baker*

Companies:
Irwin's Bakery, Portadown
Mother's Pride, Northern Ireland – Alan B Stephens
Neill's Flour Mill – Bill Cleland
Sunblest Bakeries – Alan Hempton

Elsie Berner
David Bigger
Pat Brennan
Noel Brown
Francis Dickson
Louie Dougan
Wesley Geddis
Mary Goodrich
John Halliday
The Hamill family
John Hanna
Roddy Hegarty
Helen Henderson (neé Baine)
Father Hugh Kennedy
James Kerr
John Lavery & family
Charles & Jean Ludlow
Jack Magee
John McCabe
Tom McDonald
Annette McDonnell
Harry Mulholland
Peter Radcliffe
Victor Sefton
Paul Stewart
Cecil (Junior) Whaley
Elliot Wilson